The Best of Me from a-z!

Traits and Virtues for Kids

By Mary M. Rensberry

Illustrated by Sara Murtas

from the Everyday Series Collection

The Best of Me from a-z!
    Traits and Virtues for Kids
        from the Everyday Series Collection
© 2018 by Mary Rensberry
Illustrated by Sara Murtas

ISBN-13: 978-1-940736-41-9

QuickTurtle Books LLC®
330 Schmid Rd
Fairview, MI 48621

Printed in the United States of America.

Dedication

To my grandchildren
Aden, Otto and Nola

Today...

I AM able!

I AM beautiful!

I AM creative!

I AM determined!

I AM ethical!

I AM free!

I AM generous!

I AM happy!

I AM interested!

I AM joyful!

I AM kind!

I AM loving!

I AM mannerly!

I AM natural!

I AM observant!

I AM persistent!

I AM quick!

I AM responsible!

I AM spiritual!

I AM tolerant!

I AM unique!

I AM victorious!

I AM willing!

I AM exuberant!

I AM youthful!

I AM zealous!

Definitions of the Traits & Virtues as a Guide for Parents, Teachers and Students

able-a "can do" attitude

beautiful-pleasing to the senses

creative-having original ideas of your own

determined-setting your mind to do something

ethical-knowing right from wrong

free-helping myself or others in life

generous-willing to share with another

happy-the overcoming of obstacles in life

interested-paying attention

joyful-being filled with gladness or happiness

kind-doing good rather than harm

loving-a feeling of fondness and
friendship

mannerly-to show appreciation or one's
thankfulness or gratitude in situations

natural-true to your nature

observant-able to look and see things how
they really are

persistent-being able to carry on despite all
obstacles to reach your goals

quick-to think fast

responsible-trustworthy, accountable

spiritual-caring for things of the soul or
spirit which is the cause of inspiration
and energy

tolerant-willing to look at other viewpoints
different than your own

unique-one of a kind

victorious-achieving in life what you intended

willing-cheerfully ready to help out

eXuberant-having an abundance of cheer

youthful-fresh and lively

zealous-eager and full of zeal or enthusiasm

Note to the Reader

This little book of traits and virtues is for young students in life. It gives encouragement to all readers alike to live a life more abundant and successful.

For the teacher and parent, a GAME of Virtues can be played with the student or child thinking of other <u>positive</u> words for each letter of the alphabet.

For example, for the letter a-instead of able, the word aware or active would be good virtues or attributes to have or cultivate. And so on....The list is endless! Then, for added enjoyment, act out the virtues and see if the others can guess which virtue it is.

The main thing is to have fun and enjoy being the person who you were truly created to be thus helping this world to be a better and happier place to live.

Be sure to check out some of the other books by QuickTurtle Books LLC® found on Amazon

1. Monster Monster-about a child's imagination at night
2. If I Were a Garden-a children's book of rhyme about being in the garden
3. I AM Spirit/The ABC's of an Ideal Spirit-using positive messages for encouragement
4. Christmas Christmas Everyday-From the Everyday Series Collection® about sharing the Christmas spirit each day
5. How the Snake Got Its Tail-about living a clean life free of drugs
6. Colors Talk-about the colors of the rainbow and what they say
7. If I Were a Lighthouse-A Rhyme for Young Readers about what lighthouses do to help others
8. I Wish It Were Christmas-about a tree wanting to share its gifts to the world
9. Goblin's Goop-a modern day Battle of Jericho story about the environmental evils of pesticides and the company who makes them
10. If I Were a Book-about what joys a book brings to those that read
11. If I Were a Heart-a child's book of rhyme about a loving heart
12. The Blind Dove-(The Wings of God)-a book about having a disability but yet having other gifts that most people do not use.

Made in the USA
Middletown, DE
23 April 2019